Series / Number 03-011

Minimizing Costs and Maximizing Benefits in Providing Legal Services To the Poor

STUART S. NAGEL
University of Illinois

⑤SAGE PUBLICATIONS / Beverly Hills / London

For information address:

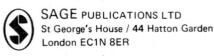

SAGE PUBLICATIONS, INC.
275 South Beverly Drive
Beverly Hills, California 90212

SAGE PUBLICATIONS LTD
St George's House / 44 Hatton Garden
London EC1N 8ER

International Standard Book Number 0-8039-0296-4

Library of Congress Catalog Card No. 73-84163

FIRST PRINTING

When citing a professional paper, please use the proper form. Remember to cite the
correct Sage Professional Paper series title and include the paper number. One of the
two following formats can be adapted (depending on the style manual used):

(1) OSTROM, E. et al. (1973) "Community Organization and the Provision of Police
Services." Sage Professional Papers in Administrative and Policy Studies, 1, 03-001.
Beverly Hills and London: Sage Pubns.

OR

(2) Ostrom, Elinor, et al. 1973. *Community Organization and the Provision of Police
Services.* Sage Professional Papers in Administrative and Policy Studies, vol. 1, series
no. 03-001. Beverly Hills and London: Sage Publications.

CONTENTS

Minimizing Costs and Maximizing Benefits in Providing Legal Services To the Poor

STUART S. NAGEL
University of Illinois

I. INTRODUCTION

PURPOSES AND LITERATURE

This paper has two purposes, a general and a specific one. The general purpose is to describe how legal policy decisions involving the allocation of scarce resources can be optimized, or at least improved upon, through the application of some simple, easy-to-understand concepts of linear regression analysis combined with linear programming, and also nonlinear regression analysis combined with differential calculus. The specific purpose is to describe the application of the above model to the optimum allocation of budgets of the legal services agencies of the Office of Economic Opportunity between routine case handling versus broader law reform work.

The linear programming methodology emphasized here has been well developed by mathematicians (Llewellyn, 1962; Vajada, 1961). It has received wide application to business and economic problems (Baumol, 1965; Richmond, 1968; Wagner, 1969). There have also been works calling for its increased use in political policy problems (Black, 1968; McKean, 1958), but there have been few applications in areas other than defense

AUTHOR'S NOTE: *This research is one of a series of policy science studies on measuring and achieving affects of alternative legal policies partly financed by National Science Foundation grant GS-2875 and the University of Illinois Research Board. Neither agency, however, is responsible for the results. The author also thanks* strategy.[1] As yet there seems to have been no published application of linear programming methodology to a problem involving decisions as to what should be the law on a controversial legal issue or how the law might be best implemented.[2]

There has been a substantial literature developed concerning evaluations of the OEO Legal Services Program (Stumpf, 1973; Catholic Lawyer, 1968; HEW, 1964; Kettelle Corp., 1971). The literature includes a running debate over the relative effort that should be allocated to case handling versus law reform (Baldwin, 1972; Agnew, 1972; Klaus, 1972; Jarmel, 1972: 3-1, 3-19; Semmel, 1970: 56-69).[3] Unfortunately, most of the allocation-debate literature tends to the somewhat emotional and lacking in quantitative data with regard either to how the effort is empirically allocated in various types of agencies or to how the empirical effort ought to be allocated in light of given goals.

DATA

From 1969 to 1972 the Urban Institute of Washington and the Auerbach and Kettelle corporations of Philadelphia prepared and applied objective evaluation forms for evaluating the work of over 200 legal services agencies across the country (Duffy et al., 1970; Auerbach Corp., 1971; Kettelle Corp., 1971). Teams of expert evaluators representing diverse perspectives were chosen under the supervision of the Office of Legal Services.[4] They spent at least a few days in each agency conducting many interviews and observing procedures to determine on a structured scale how each agency scored on over a hundred different rating criteria (including one overall rating), as well as many cost and background variables. The total cost of this massive data gathering was approximately $1,500,000. In this article, this data base provides the raw material for illustrating the linear programming methodology for choosing between case handling and law reform legal services activities.

The Auerbach data provides complete information for 51 unnamed legal services agencies with regard to the following basic variables used in this analysis: (1) the total budget per year for each agency, symbolized B; (2) the total planned participants per year, symbolized P; (3) the percentage of law reform and related activities other than routine case

Roger Detweiler and Fred Baldwin of the Office of Economic Opportunity for access to data on the Legal Services Program, and Marian Neef, Secil Tuncalp, and Tony Champagne of the University of Illinois for their assistance in processing the data. The reader should see the notes at the back of this article for further explanation and justification of the methods used.

handling,[5] symbolized %L, and (4) the overall project rating or satisfaction score, symbolized S.

From these four variables, one can create the four transformed variables needed for the linear programming analysis. First, the number of dollars spent per participant[6] for law reform (symbolized $L) equals %L times B/P. Second, the number of dollars spent per participant for case handling (symbolized $C) equals (100% − %L) times B/P. Third, the number of dollars spent per participant in total equals B/P or $L + $C. Fourth, S (meaning project satisfaction) can range from a low of 1 to a high of 12.[7]

The Kettelle data provides complete information on the four basic variables for only 16 agencies as contrasted to the Auerbach 51 agencies. Because the Kettelle data is based on a smaller sample, it will not be used in this article as much as the Auerbach data. It will, however, be occasionally referred to at least in the footnotes bacause it does provide an additional sample of agencies, it provides more meaningful measurement on some of the variables, and the raw Kettelle data is more readily available to the general public.[8]

Two of the 51 agencies were eliminated from the analysis of the Auerbach data because they were so deviant from the average agency with regard to dollars spent per participant.[9] Without those two deviant agencies, the average agency spent a total amount of $68.34 per participant, $62.18 (or 91 percent) on case handling and $6.16 (or 9 percent) on law reform.[10] The two deviant cases spent a total amount per participant of $633.94 and $294.20, respectively.[11]

The especially interesting question is not how much money did the average agency actually spend for case handling and for law reform, but rather how much money should the average agency spend for case handling and law reform in order to minimize costs at a given satisfaction level or to maximize satisfaction at a given cost level? That type of question is what the rest of this paper is designed to answer.

BASIC CONCEPTS

The methodology for making an optimum choice between activity variables depends on whether the dollars spent for each activity produce a constant change or increase in satisfaction or benefits (the constant returns situation), or whether dollars spent produce an increase in satisfaction but at a decreasing rate (the diminishing returns situation). Constant returns can be thought of as a straight line relation between dollars spent and satisfaction obtained, whereas diminishing returns represent a curved line or logarithmic relation between expenditures and satisfaction. The constant returns assumption enables one to use linear regression and linear programming to find the optimum allocation, whereas the diminishing returns assumption (which is more empirically realistic) may require the use of nonlinear regression and differential calculus to optimize the allocation. These terms will all be defined and explained without assuming any prior knowledge more sophisticated than high school algebra.

Optimizing programming can be defined as a procedure whereby one finds the optimum allocation of something between two or more alternatives in light of a given minimizing or maximizing goal (called the objective function) and in light of given constraints or conditions. In order to be linear rather than nonlinear programming, both the goal and the constraints must involve only relations between variables that are straight-line or constant return relations, as previously mentioned.

In any policy-making problem involving the allocation of scarce resources to two or more activities,[12] the generalized normative constraints or desired conditions will be as follows:

(1) The minimum level for alternative activity number one which the allocation *should* allow.

(2) The maximum level for alternative number one which the allocation should allow.

(3) The minimum level for alternative number two (and so on for additional alternatives).

(4) The maximum level for alternative number two (and so on for additional alternatives).

(5) The minimum total cost. (The minimum is generally the sum of the minimums for each alternative activity.)

(6) The maximum total cost. (The maximum is generally the total budget available.)

(7) An equation showing how each activity relates to the total cost. Total cost = Activity 1 + Activity 2.

(8) The minimum benefit level.

(9) The maximum benefit level.

(10) An equation showing how each activity relates to the total benefits. Total benefits = Benefits with zero cost + (Weight 1 · Activity 1) + (Weight 2 · Activity 2).

In a policy-making problem involving possible costs and possible benefits, one might seek to:

(1) Minimize costs at a given benefit level.

(2) Maximize benefits at a given cost level.

(3) Maximize benefits minus costs.

What follows involves a more detailed explanation of these basic concepts, particularly as applied to the legal services allocation problem.

II. CHOOSING AMONG LEGAL SERVICES ACTIVITIES ASSUMING A CONSTANT RETURN TO DOLLARS SPENT

CONSTRAINTS OR CONDITIONS TO SATISFY

Nonbenefit Constraints

Figure 1 graphically shows all of the ten constraints involved in the legal services problem for the average legal services agency in the Auerbach data sample. For the first constraint, the minimum desired level for law reform activity for the average agency is $6.83 out of the total budget of $68.34 per participant. This figure was arrived at by taking 10 percent of the total budget in view of the fact that 10 percent seems to be the minimum desired allocation of the evaluators.[13] The maximum level for law reform activity which the allocation should allow is $13.67 or 20 percent of the total budget. This percentage corresponds to the highest category on which the variable was scored that described the percentage of effort devoted to law reform.[14]

For the third constraint, the minimum desired level for case handling activity in the average agency is $54.67 out of the total budget of $68.34 per participant. This figure was arrived at by taking 80 percent of the total budget in view of the fact that if law reform can constitute only a maximum of 20 percent, then case handling must constitute a minimum of 80 percent. The maximum level for case handling activity which the allocation should allow is $61.50 or 90 percent of the total budget.[15] This percentage corresponds to the fact that if law reform must constitute a minimum of 10 percent, then case handling must not constitute more than 90 percent.

The minimum total cost is $61.50. This is arrived at by summing the minimum $L which is $6.83 and the minimum $C which is $54.67. If the alternative activities had no minimum expenditures other than zero dollars and our only goal was to minimize costs regardless of satisfaction obtained, then spending zero dollars would be the optimal solution. There is no way of spending negative dollars. The graph, however, does not show the point where zero law reform dollars and zero case handling dollars are spent because the graph begins at the $46 level of case handling since none of the constraint lines are drawn in the region below $46 of case handling.

For the sixth constraint, the maximum total cost per average agency is $68.34. This maximum cost constraint is shown by the diagonal line

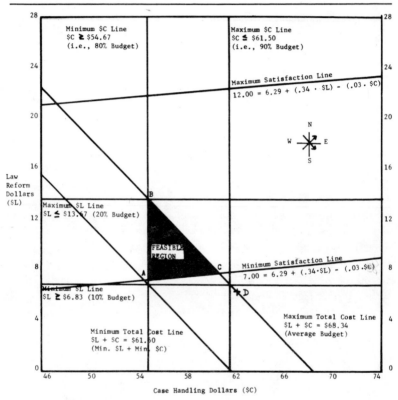

Point A is where total cost is minimized within the constraints.
　　$L = $7.06. $C = $54.67. %C = $61.74. S = 7.00.
Point B is where satisfaction is maximized within the constraints.
　　$L = $13.67. $C = $54.67. TC = $68.34. S = 9.27.
Point C is where total cost is maximized and satisfaction is minimized within the constraints.
　　$L = $7.46. $C = $60.88. TC = $68.34. S = 7.00.
Point D is where the average LSP agency in the survey is.
　　$L = $6.16. $C = $62.18. TC = $68.34. S = 6.51.
All dollar amounts refer to dollars per planned participant.

Figure 1: Allocating $L and $C to Minimize Costs or Maximize Benefits (with constant returns)

running from northwest to southeast. At its southeast extremity, the line indicates that if zero dollars were spent on law reform, $68.34 from the total budget could be spent on case handling or vice versa. At its northwest extremity, the line indicates that if $46 were spent on case handling, $22.34 from the total budget could be spent on law reform or vice versa. Once those two points are connected by a straight line, any point along the diagonal straight line involves an allocation of law reform dollars and case handling dollars that add up to $68.34. This line is sometimes called an equal cost line because the total costs at any point on the line are equal, or it is sometimes called a consumption possibility line because it indicates the total amount of money available to be consumed.

That maximum line, like the minimum total cost line, also represents one version of the equation involved in constraint seven. The general version of constraint 7 is $L + $C equals total cost. Total cost, however, does not necessarily have to be the total budget since the total cost can range from zero dollars on up to $68.34.

Benefit Constraints

The minimum total benefit level desired by the evaluators seems to be a rating score of 7.00, or 7 units of satisfaction, because a project below that level is referred to as a "project [that] has internal problems [and] requires technical assistance," whereas a project at that level is referred to as a "project operating efficiently."[16] The maximum total benefit level is a rating score of 12.00, or 12 units of satisfaction, because the rating scale did not allow for the possibility of any ratings higher than 12.00. In order to show the minimum benefit level of 7.00 or the maximum benefit level of 12.00 on Figure 1, it is necessary to understand how to derive a constraint 10 equation showing how each activity relates to the total benefits.

If we wanted to draw a straight line depicting an equation relating law reform dollars spent and satisfaction obtained, we could plot on a two-dimensional graph 49 dots corresponding to the 49 legal services agencies for which we have complete information in the Auerbach data. Each dot shows for each agency (1) how many dollars it spent for law reform per participant as indicated by the position of the dot relative to the horizontal axis and (2) how many units of satisfaction it provided to the diverse evaluators as indicated by the position of the dot relative to the vertical axis.

Through algebraic means, one can fit a line to those dots that will minimize the square of the distances from the dots to the line. This regression line can then be expressed as an equation with the form $S = a + (b \cdot \$L)$. The "a" geometrically represents the distance from the zero point to the point where the line crosses the vertical axis, and in economic terms it represents the number of units of satisfaction obtained without spending any law reform dollars. The "b" geometrically represents the degree to which the line slopes, and in economic terms it represents the ratio between a change in $\$L$ and the corresponding change in S. A similar regression line can be constructed to show the relation between $\$C$ and S. Likewise, these two regression lines can be combined into one multiple regression line showing the relation between both $\$L$ and $\$C$ simultaneously related to S with the overlap between $\$L$ and $\$C$ statistically removed. Such a multiple regression line[17] can be expressed as a constraint 10 equation having the form $S = a + (b_1 \cdot \$L) + (b_2 \cdot \$C)$.

When the above regression analysis is carried out by hand or with a computer with the 49 legal services agencies, the regression equation relating $\$L$ and S is $S = 4.67 + (.29 \cdot \$L)$, and the regression equation relating $\$C$ and S is $S = 7.58 - (.02 \cdot \$C)$. These figures indicate that $\$L$ has a positive correlation with satisfaction obtained, but $\$C$ has a negative correlation with satisfaction obtained.[18] Many of the evaluators were present or former legal services attorneys, law professors, lawyers, social work administrators, and community analysts who favor a more broadly effective legal services program in terms of improving the conditions of the poor. It is therefore understandable that money spent for law reform might tend to satisfy such evaluators more than money spent for case handling. It is, however, not so easy to understand why money spent for case handling would produce a negative or inverse correlation with satisfaction obtained rather than just a lower correlation.

One further explanation for why additional dollars spent on case handling might correlate with decreased satisfaction is that additional case handling activity may empirically mean reduced law reform activity, thereby producing reduced satisfaction (although both $\$C$ and $\$L$ can theoretically increase or be high).[19] Another explanation is that the cities where the most case handling dollars per participant are being spent are those cities that had especially explosive low satisfaction or high dissatisfaction to begin with in the middle 1960s when OEO legal services began, thereby causing extra money to be spent on them, including $\$C$. In other words, the low satisfaction caused the high spending rather than the reverse. In fact, if data over time could be obtained, one might find that in the high spending areas, the satisfaction has increased although it is still lower than in the low spending areas.[20] As an additional explanation, perhaps increased spending may also produce rising expectations or rising standards such that satisfaction goes down because the standards set by the evaluators have gone up faster than the achievement. It seems unlikely that increased case handling expenditures in themselves would produce lowered satisfaction.[21]

When the above-mentioned multiple regression analysis is carried out, the constraint 10 regression equation relating $L and $C simultaneously to S is S = 6.29 + (.34 · $L) − (.03 · $C). This regression equation yields a multiple correlation coefficient of .78 out of a possible 1.00 correlation. If we set S equal to the minimum S of 7.00, then we can plot constraint 8 showing what combinations of $L and $C will achieve a rating of 7.00. Given this multiple regression equation with S = 7.00, then by simple algebra and arithmetic, one can see that $L = (.09 · $C) + $2.09, and $C = (11.33 · $L) − $23.67. We then find any two points on this equation line and connect the two points to determine the equation line. For example, we can find that the value of $L is $6.23 when $C = $46.00, and that the value of $C is $66.97 when $L = $8.00. This yields a minimum benefit line with a slight slope from the southwest to the northeast.

Likewise, if we set S equal to the maximum S of 12.00, then we can plot constraint 9, showing what combinations of $L and $C will achieve a rating of 12.00. Given the above multiple regression equation with S = 12.00, one can see that $L = (.09 · $C) + $16.80, and $C = (11.33 · $L) − $190.33. This line can be plotted by finding two points on it, such as the point corresponding to an $L of $23.00 and a $C of $70.26, and the point corresponding to a $C of $46.00 and a $L of $20.94. This yields a maximum benefit line also with a slight slope from southwest to the northeast which is parallel to, but higher than, the minimum satisfaction line.[22]

Both the minimum and maximum benefit lines are sometimes called equal benefit, equal product, or indifference lines because the benefits obtained by any allocation corresponding to a point on either line are equal to any other point on that line. Like equal cost lines, equal benefit lines normally slope from northwest to southeast (although not with the same slope), meaning that a reduction in expenditure on one activity requires an increase in expenditure on the other activity in order to hold constant the total benefits (or the total costs in the case of an equal cost line). Both the Auerbach and the Kettelle data, however, indicate equal benefit lines which have a positive (rather than an inverse) relation between $L and $C, meaning (1) when there is an increase in $L, there has to be an increase in $C in order to keep the total benefits from rising, and (2) when there is a decrease in $L, there has to be a decrease in $C in order to keep the total benefits from falling. This relation follows from the fact that $L correlates positively with satisfaction, and $C correlates negatively with satisfaction, as previously mentioned. If one could obtain data to statistically control for: (1) the prior satisfaction level before the increase in $C, and (2) the change in standards or rising expectations, then both $L and $C might correlate positively with satisfaction, and the equal benefit line would have an inverse slope from northwest to southeast rather than a positive slope from southwest to northeast.

Regardless of which way any of the lines in Figure 1 slope, the optimization techniques of linear programming are applicable so long as the lines block off a closed surface of the figure in which the optimum allocation point must lie. It is those optimization techniques to which we now turn.

GOALS TO OPTIMIZE

When the above ten constraints are determined, one can then easily determine the optimum allocation between the activity variables in order to minimize costs or maximize benefits, either graphically or through the use of a computer.

Minimizing Costs

If one wants to minimize total costs while obtaining the minimum satisfaction level of 7.00, then from Figure 1, one can see that point A will involve the optimum allocation between law reform dollars and case handling dollars. This is the point where the minimum satisfaction line intersects the minimum $C line, slightly above the minimum $L line. At this point, $C equals $54.67, and $L equals $7.07. If one plugs those values of $C and $L into the regression equation given in constraint 10, then those values will produce a satisfaction level of exactly 7.00.[23] Note that the optimum cost line through point A is not the same as the minimum cost line, which is just below point A, because the minimum cost line is below the minimum satisfaction line at point A, meaning no feasible combination of $L and $C adding up to only the minimum cost will give a satisfaction level of 7.00.[24]

The sum of the values for $C and $L is only $61.74, representing a saving of $6.60 from the $68.34 total budget available. This average savings of $6.60 per participant per legal services agency adds up to a large sum of money available for establishing additional legal services agencies if one multiplies the $6.60 by the total number of Legal Services Program participants across the country. The average agency in the Auerbach sample of 201 agencies had 3,369 participants. Given the fact that in 1970 there were about 300 legal services agencies across the country, this would mean more than 1,000,000 participants in the total program. A million participants times a savings of over $6.00 per participant means a savings of more than $6,000,000 which was more than 10 percent of the $58,000,000 total national budget for the OEO Legal Services Program in 1970.[25] This follows from the fact that a $6.60 saving per participant represents about 10 percent of the $68.34 available per participant. With the additional $6,000,000, many communities in need of legal services agencies could be provided with them.

The reason point A represents the optimum cost-minimization point is because it is the point on the minimum satisfaction line that is farthest away from the maximum cost line and yet not below either the minimum $C line or the minimum $L line. Any allocation point closer to the maximum cost line would waste money, even though it would be within the feasible region where all the minimum and maximum constraints are satisfied. Likewise, any allocation point farther from the maximum cost line would fail to satisfy the minimum constraints on S and $C, and ultimately on $L and total cost.

Instead of saying the cost-minimization point is to spend $54.67 on case handling per participant and $7.07 on law reform in order to obtain a satisfaction level of 7.00, it would generally be more meaningful to state the proper allocation in terms of percentages. The optimum percentage of an agency's budget to allocate to $C should be 80 percent because that is the minimum percent that can be allocated to $C. One should not allocate more than 80 percent to $C because doing so will either reduce satisfaction, as the Auerbach and Kettelle data indicate, or will at least probably not increase it as much as using the extra money for law reform.

.The total remaining 20 percent of the budget should not be allocated to law reform, however, if one wants to minimize costs with a minimum satisfaction level since less than a 20 percent allocation will achieve the minimum 7.00 satisfaction. The exact percentage to allocate to $L will vary for each agency somewhere between 10 percent (the minimum $L) and 20 percent (the maximum $L), depending on the agency's total budget. To determine the exact percentage to allocate to $L, (1) calculate 80 percent of the total budget to determine $C, (2) plug that figure in place of $C in the combined constraint 8 and 10 formula $7.00 = 6.29 + (.34 \cdot \$L) - (.03 \cdot \$C)$, (3) solve for $L, and (4) divide this solution of $L by the total budget to determine the percentage of the total budget to allocate to $L.

If one wants to talk in terms of allocating the 1970 national budget of

$58,000,000 to $L and $C rather than allocating the average agency budget, one should spend 80 percent of the national budget on $C and at least 10 percent of the national budget on $L. The exact percent to spend on $L should equal the sum of the $L figures calculated by the above four-step process for each agency, divided by $58,000,000. The same above percentages could be applied to the 1971 national budget provided that the Legal Services Program continued to set a minimum of about 80 percent on $C and about 10 percent on $L.

If in step 4 the value of $L for a given agency comes out to be less than 10 percent of the total budget (as might happen with an especially large budget per participant), then spend exactly 10 percent on $L. Doing so will satisfy the minimum $L constraint and at the same time satisfy the minimum benefit constraint, although the satisfaction level produced may be higher than 7.00. This is all right because the minimum benefit constraint does not require that *only* the minimum benefits be obtained, but rather that *at least* the minimum benefits be obtained.[26] If, however, in step 4 above the value of $L comes out to be more than 20 percent of the total budget (as might happen with an especially small budget), then one cannot spend exactly 20 percent on $L and still satisfy the 7.00 satisfaction level.[27] In other words, it is possible to devise a set of inconsistent constraints that cannot be satisfied simultaneously. Graphically, this means having a set of constraints that do not produce a closed feasible region in which the optimum allocation points can lie.

One especially interesting thing to note from Figure 1, which is of value in minimizing costs below point A, is that we could further lower the costs without lowering the satisfaction if we could decrease only the minimum $C constraint line (which automatically decreases the minimum total cost line). For example, if we were to lower the $C from $54.67 to $46.00, we could still obtain a 7.00 satisfaction level by spending $46.00 for $C and $6.23 for $L or an optimum total cost of $52.23 which would be a saving of $16.11 from the maximum total cost of $68.34 per participant. The difference between what we do save by spending at point A and what we could save by spending at a point on the minimum satisfaction line to the left of point A represents opportunity cost or lost increased optimization. Regardless of the economics, for political reasons it is unlikely that a drastic reduction in case handling will be allowed by the Office of Economic Opportunity, if it means an increase in law reform under a relatively conservative presidential administration.

Likewise, if we were willing to lower our minimum satisfaction line, we could also save some additional money although at reduced satisfaction and less than we could save by lowering the minimum $C line. Whether the saved money would offset the reduced satisfaction would depend on how many dollars one satisfaction unit is worth to the consumer-evaluators, about which more will be said later. Both the minimum $C line and the minimum satisfaction line are referred to as binding constraints in this cost minimization problem because the optimum point is pushing against the intersection of the minimum $C line and the minimum satisfaction line. Binding constraints, and only binding constraints, raise the possibility of opportunity costs and of increased optimization by changing the constraints. Nonbinding constraints may become binding if the former binding constraints are changed, as would happen to the minimum $L line if the minimum satisfaction line were substantially lowered.

An alternative way of interpreting the cost minimization in Figure 1, which is related to production and consumption economics, is to say that the point of cost minimization is the point where a line running below and parallel to the maximum cost line will be exactly tangential to the feasible region. What we are then saying is that constraint 7 defines a family of parallel equal cost lines, one of which represents the optimum cost line. The optimum cost line, however, must be within or at least touching the feasible region where all the constraints are simultaneously satisfied. Such an optimum cost position exists only at point A. This point can be thought of as the point where the government producer of legal services minimizes its total costs in allocating its budget to two factors of production, namely law reform and case handling, analogous to labor and capital.[28]

Maximizing Benefits

Instead of minimizing costs at a given satisfaction level, Figure 1 can be used to maximize benefits at a given total cost level. Thus, if one wants to keep total costs at or below the maximum cost level of $68.34 and yet maximize satisfaction, point B will involve the optimum allocation between law reform dollars and case handling dollars. This is the point where the maximum cost line intersects both the maximum $L line and the minimum $C line. At this point, $C equals $54.67, and $L equals $13.67, consuming the total $68.34 budget.[29] If one plugs those values of $C and $L into the regression equation given in constraint 10, those values would produce a satisfaction level of exactly 9.27.

The average level of satisfaction for the 49 agencies used from the Auerbach data was only 6.45 because the agencies were not optimally allocating their funds between law reform and case handling. With the above-described benefit-maximization allocation causing the satisfaction level to rise to 9.27, there would be a gain of 2.82 satisfaction units, or a 44 percent gain. To have the Legal Services Program or any governmental program produce 44 percent more satisfaction without spending additional money, by merely reallocating its expenditures, seems to be a change worth adopting, or at least worth looking into.

The reason point B represents the optimum cost maximization point is because it is the point on the maximum cost line that is farthest away from the minimum satisfaction line and yet not beyond either the maximum $L line or the minimum $C line. Any allocation point closer to the minimum satisfaction line would involve less satisfaction even though it would be within the feasible region where all the minimum and maximum constraints are satisfied. Likewise, any allocation point farther from the minimum satisfaction line would fail to satisfy the constraints on $C, $L, and possibly on S as well if one moves above the maximum S line.

Instead of saying the benefit maximization point is to spend $54.67 on case handling per participant and $13.67 for law reform, it would generally be more meaningful to state the proper allocation in terms of percentages. The optimum percentage of an agency's budget to allocate to $C should be 80 percent since that is the minimum percent that can be allocated. The remaining 20 percent of the budget should all be allocated to law reform if one wishes to maximize total satisfaction rather than to save some of the budget. These same percentages apply to the 1970 national budget of $58,000,000 if one wants to talk in terms of allocating that national budget to $L and $C rather than allocating the average agency budget.

If allocating the remaining 20 percent of an agency's budget to $L results in producing more than the maximum 12.00 possible satisfaction (as might happen with an especially large agency budget per participant), then only as much $L as is needed to bring satisfaction up to the maximum S level need be spent.[30] To determine this optimum $L short of 20 percent, (1) calculate 80 percent of the budget available to satisfy the minimum $C constraint, (2) plug that figure into the combined constraint 9 and 10 formula $12.00 = 6.29 + (.34 \cdot \$L) - (.03 \cdot \$C)$ in place of $C, (3) solve for $L, and (4) divide this solution of $L by the total budget to determine the percentage of the total budget to allocate to $L.

As the cost minimization analysis, Figure 1 reveals the presence of opportunity costs that keep down benefit maximization. Note that if the maximum $L line could be raised, substantially greater satisfaction benefits could be obtained at the same maximum cost level. Likewise, the mimimum $C line (which is the complement of the maximum $L line) could be lowered to produce greater satisfaction benefits at the same maximum cost level. The maximum cost line also represents a binding constraint. However, if it is raised (unlike raising maximum $L and lowering minimum $C), the total costs will be raised. This means one would have to decide whether the additional units of satisfaction are worth the additional units of cost.

An alternative way of interpreting the benefit maximization in Figure 1 that is related to consumption and production economics is to say that the point of benefit maximization is the point where a line running above and parallel to the minimum satisfaction line would be exactly tangential to the feasible region. What we are then saying is that constraint number 10 defines a family of parallel equal benefit lines, one of which represents the optimum benefit line. That optimum benefit line, however, must be within, or at least tangential to, the feasible region where all the constraints are simultaneously satisfied. Such an optimum benefit position exists only at point B. This point can be thought of as the point where the government, representing consumers of legal services, maximizes their total utility by allocating their collective budget to two consumer goods, namely law reform and case handling, analogous to food and clothing.[31]

Optimizing Other Goals

Perhaps there are other meaningful goals that could be optimized besides minimizing total costs or maximizing total benefits. One can of course change the constraints while keeping the same goals or objective functions. This was done between the Auerbach data and the Kettelle data with regard to changing the maximum percent of the budget that could be devoted to law reform. Likewise, the equal benefit equation expressed in constraint 10 could be changed if empirical data were available on some of the intervening variables (like prior satisfaction and rising expectations) which may be interfering with the true relation between case handling and satisfaction.

Point C within the feasible region at first glance looks as if it might be an optimum point for something. More careful examination, however, indicates that it is the point where total costs are maximized at a minimum level of satisfaction or where total benefits are minimized at maximum total cost. No rational producer or consumer would have as a goal to maximize costs irrespective of satisfaction or to minimize satisfaction irrespective of costs. Likewise, it is not rational in terms of getting the most for one's money to seek to maximize $L or $C or to minimize $L or $C irrespective of the effect on total costs or total satisfaction. Thus, the only rational goal optimization involving a single variable is to minimize costs subject to the satisfaction constraints or to maximize satisfaction subject to the total cost constraints.

However, what about minimizing or maximizing some combination of variables? More specifically, what about maximizing total satisfaction minus total costs (which is the same thing as minimizing total costs minus total satisfaction). To maximize satisfaction minus costs sounds like maximizing profits since profits equal benefits or revenue minus costs. This also sounds like an ideal way to combine cost minimization and benefit maximization and thereby avoid having to choose between those two goals. So long as satisfaction and costs are measured on two different dimensions, however, one cannot subtract one from the other. To do so would be like subtracting hours from pounds or typewriters from miles. It is also like subtracting three oranges from two crates of oranges. To express the answer or the remainder in terms of oranges or crates, one has to know how many oranges are in a crate. To express the answer in money or in some other medium of exchange, one must translate both oranges and crates into dollars or other monetary units.

If benefits were measured in dollars instead of satisfaction units and costs were also measured in dollars, the problem would be quite simple and the optimum allocation of $L and $C to maximize satisfaction minus costs would be either at point A or at point B. It can be proved that, in any linear programming problem, the optimum solution must always be at a corner point within the feasible region, assuming there is a feasible region (Kemeny et al., 1959: 249-259; Baumol, 1965: 79-84). Corner point C can be eliminated as being irrational since it maximizes cost and minimizes satisfaction. This only leaves corner points A and B.

At corner point A the total satisfaction is 7.00, and the total cost is $61.75. At corner point B the total satisfaction is 9.27, and the total cost is $68.34. Corner point A rather than B maximizes satisfaction minus cost if each satisfaction unit is worth only $1.00. This is so because $7.00 in benefits minus $61.75 in costs means a loss of only $54.75, whereas $9.27 in benefits minus $68.34 in costs means a larger loss of $59.07. On the other hand, if each satisfaction unit is worth $10.00, then point B rather than A maximizes satisfaction minus cost, because $70.00 minus $61.75 means a profit of only $8.25, whereas $92.70 minus $68.34 means a larger profit of $24.36. Obviously, whether point A or point B is the point of minimum losses or maximum profits depends on how many dollars one satisfaction unit is worth.

Unfortunately, there is no meaningful way of determining how much one satisfaction unit is worth in terms of dollars from the data available.

Methods have been suggested for converting nonmonetary consumer values into monetary ones, but they all involve rather sophisticated surveying of the evaluators, and this was not done when the evaluation studies were made by the Auerbach or Kettelle management consultant firms (Baumol, 1965: 211-217, 512-528; Miller and Starr, 1960: 65-72). In the legal services problem, it is the benefits that are nonmonetary, while the costs are monetary. In environmental protection problems, by way of contrast, the social costs are partly nonmonetary aesthetic costs, and the benefits (such as electric power) are often capable of monetary measurement.[32] Perhaps in the future, governmental agencies in making evaluation studies will seek to use the methods available for determining the demand curve or indifference curve between nonmonetary units and dollars so as to facilitate subsequent policy analysis designed to maximize benefits minus costs.[33]

If one cannot combine cost minimization and benefit maximization by maximizing benefits minus costs, then one must choose between these conflicting goals. The main advantage of minimizing costs is to have some money left over from the budget which can be used for expansion of the program beyond what was originally contemplated. This may be especially important in legal services work since there are so many communities in the country which need a legal services agency, but there are virtually no funds available for expanding the number of agencies as contrasted to just maintaining the existing ones at their present levels of operation. It also seems wasteful to spend more than the number of dollars needed to obtain a minimum level of satisfaction, especially if additional spending produces diminishing returns or diminishing utility. If the government is mainly viewed as a producer of services, then the government should seek to minimize the cost of production by choosing the optimum combination of production factors the way a manufacturer does.

On the other hand, it may be quite unrealistic to expect local agencies to return the savings they obtained from a more rational allocation of dollars to law reform and case handling while maintaining the existing level of satisfaction. It is unrealistic because local agencies fear that if they save portions of their budget, next year's budget will be substantially reduced or at least not increased. It may also be unrealistic because agencies will tend to find a way of spending the savings on themselves rather than returning the savings for use by other less efficient agencies. The more meaningful approach may therefore be to allow each agency to spend all of its budget while trying to persuade it to divide it between law reform and case handling in such a way as to provide maximum satisfaction or benefits. One can also try to cut the potential savings out of agency budgets in advance and encourage them to use the remaining budget to maximum efficiency so as to maintain the same level of satisfaction as existed under the former higher budget. In addition, if the government is mainly viewed as a consumer of services, then the government should seek to maximize the utility of its purchases by choosing the optimum combination of products the way a rational consumer theoretically does.

Although one cannot (1) simultaneously minimize costs and maximize benefits or (2) maximize benefits minus costs, one can arrive at a compromise position between minimizing costs and maximizing benefits. Thus with the data from Figure 1, one can choose an $L of $10.37 which is the midpoint between $7.07 (the cost minimization position) and $13.67 (the benefit maximization position). Doing so will mean a compromise $C of $54.67, TC of $65.04, and S of 8.18. The $C remains at minimum $C in this compromise; TC remains the sum of $L and $C; and the new S can be calculated accurately enough by interpolation between the S at the cost minimization position and the S at the benefit maximization position.

Ultimately, the choice between these two alternative strategies, or a compromise between them, depends on the nature of the problem and especially on the values of the evaluators or the policy makers who have hired the evaluators. One criticism that might be levied against the satisfaction ratings in the Auerbach and Kettelle data is that the evaluators there were not representative in their values of some group for which the critic has a high regard. The evaluators, however, were chosen, at least indirectly, by high level officials in the Office of Economic Opportunity, who were themselves appointed by the president and approved by congress, who are in turn chosen by the general electorate. Unfortunately, although those evaluators may reflect representative values as of 1969 when the evaluation began, those 1969 values may no longer prevail. Anyone seeking to make use of an evaluative policy analysis must of course consider by whom and when the evaluations were made.

Before leaving the section on choosing between legal activities while assuming a constant or linear return to dollars spent, it should be pointed out that no matter what goals one seeks to optimize in a linear programming problem, there are now canned or previously prepared computer programs available for doing the arithmetic work involved. The arithmetic was fairly simple for Figure 1 and could be carried out by hand or with a desk calculator, but linear programming problems can be devised for which a computer is quite helpful. This is especially so if (1) the constraints establish numerous corner points in the feasible region or (2) there are more than two activity variables involved, thereby producing a three-dimensional or N-dimensional figure. However, a problem with N activity variables can be simplified by grouping the activities together to form two groups of M and N − M activities respectively. After allocating an optimum role to the M activity group and the N − M activity group, one can break each of those groups down into a pair of conflicting activities or into a pair of conflicting groups of activities.

With a canned linear programming routine, the ten constraints to satisfy and two goals to optimize are provided on twelve IBM data cards punched as follows:

$L	$C	Total Cost	S	Relation	Constant
1	0	0	0	GE	6.83
1	0	0	0	LE	13.67
0	1	0	0	GE	54.67
0	1	0	0	LE	61.50
0	0	1	0	GE	61.50
0	0	1	0	LE	68.34
1	1	−1	0	EQ	0.00
0	0	0	1	GE	7.00
0	0	0	1	LE	12.00
−.34	.03	0	1	EQ	6.29
0	0	1	0	MN	
0	0	0	1	MX	

These twelve IBM data cards are preceded by a format card informing the computer that the first four columns of data in this data matrix are (1) the first activity variable, (2) the second activity variable, (3) the total cost variable, and (4) the total benefit variable. The sixth column contains a positive number, and the fifth column shows the relation between the four variables and that number. The five possible relations are (1) greater than or equal to, (2) less than or equal to, (3) equal to, (4) minimize, or (5) maximize. The numbers in the first four columns are the coefficients of the variables in the relational equation. Card 10 is algebraically equivalent to the satisfaction-regression equation, but is written that way so that the "a" coefficient number can be on the right side of the relation term as a positive number. Preceding these twelve cards is the format card and a couple of cards identifying the user, the program call number, and the number of data cards. That's all there is to getting out of the computer the optimum values of $L, $C, total costs, and total benefits at points A and B (provided there is a feasible region), plus an analysis of the possible opportunity costs.

Unfortunately, these computer programs work only when there are solely linear or constant returns constraints in the problem in spite of the fact that diminishing returns may be more empirically realistic. How to handle a cost minimization or benefit maximization problem with diminishing returns relations between dollars spent and benefits obtained (particularly with regard to providing legal services to the poor) is the subject to which we now turn.

III. CHOOSING AMONG LEGAL SERVICES ACTIVITIES WITH DIMINISHING RETURNS AND A POSITIVELY SLOPED EQUAL BENEFIT LINE

CONSTRAINTS TO SATISFY

Constraint 10 expresses the relationship between total benefits obtained and dollars spent for each activity. As initially stated, it produces a straight satisfaction line when graphed. Such a straight line relationship may accurately reflect empirical reality over a short distance of total expenditures like an increase from $30 to $40. Over a long distance of expenditures, however, like an increase from zero dollars to $100 or more, incremental expenditures may not produce equally incremental benefits. The principle of diminishing returns or diminishing utility is a common phenomenon in that, although incremental expenditures may produce incremental benefits, they may do so at a decreasing rate. In other words, each additional unit purchased tends to produce less additional satisfaction than the previous unit because there is a lessening need for each additional unit (Samuelson, 1967: 23-26, 417-419; Baumol, 1965: 185-188, 253-255).

In view of the fact that the constant returns or straight line assumption may be realistic for many situations, and in view of the greater complexity in dealing with diminishing returns or curved line relations, one may wish to (1) skip this section, and the next, (2) not read them so thoroughly, or (3) delegate the reading of them to someone else. If, however, one has an understanding of basic algebra and little patience, one can master the potentially useful policy analysis material contained in the rest of this article. What may seem difficult at first may be quickly clarified from the graphing or from the concrete examples which are interspersed within the more general discussion.

To adjust constraint 10 to reflect this diminishing returns phenomenon, one can simply rewrite the general formula to read total benefits = (benefits with a one dollar cost) · (Activity 1 raised to the power of weight 1) · (Activity 2 raised to the power of weight 2). In terms of the algebraic symbols used in the legal services problem, the formula would be $S = a \cdot \$L^{b_1} \cdot \$C^{b_2}$. If this equation is graphed, it produces a line relating S to $L and/or $C that rises but at a decreasing rate, eventually tapering off to almost a plateau, provided that the two weights are each decimals less than one. This equation or curve is referred to as an exponential curve with decimal exponents or sometimes as a Cobb-Douglas function (Guilford, 1954: 43-78; Baumol, 1965: 14-17, 402-403).

Constraint 7 expresses the relationship between total costs and dollars spent for each activity. Unlike the original constraint 10, it always accurately reflects reality since it is true by definition of total cost that the sum of the costs of the individual activities adds up to the total cost.

Values for "a," "b_1," and "b_2" in the above curved satisfaction-line formula can be determined in a manner similar to the way those values are determined in the straight satisfaction-line formula. To do so, however, requires transforming the curved formula into a straight line by changing the multiplication signs to addition and the power exponents to multiplication without changing the meaning of the formula. Fortunately, this can be done by taking the logarithm of both sides of the equation because the $\text{Log} (Y \cdot X) = \text{Log } Y + \text{Log } X$ and $\text{Log } Y^X = X \cdot \text{Log } Y$. Therefore, taking the log of both sides of the curved satisfaction equation results in the transformed logarithmic equation $\text{Log } S = \text{Log } a + (b_1 \cdot \text{Log } \$L) + (b_2 \cdot \text{Log } \$C)$. Taking the log of a number merely means finding in a logarithmic table an exponent for the base ten such that when ten is raised to the power of that exponent, the result will equal the number whose logarithm we are seeking.[34]

It is fortunate that canned computer programs are readily available for solving the value of "a," "b_1," and "b_2" in the above logarithmic equation. All that is needed is to inform the computer for each of the 49 legal services agencies in the Auerbach data (1) how much was spent for law reform or $L, (2) how much was spent for case handling or $C, and (3) what was the agency's overall satisfaction rating, as was done in determining constraint 10 before. One then informs the computer (1) to find the logs of $L, $C, and S; (2) to in effect plot dots representing the logs of $L and $C against the log of S; (3) to fit a straight line or plane to those dots that minimizes the squares of the vertical distances from those dots to the line, (4) to determine the slope of $L to S (while statistically controlling for $C), which equals b_1; (5) to determine the slope of $C to S (while stastically controlling for $L), which equals b_2; and (6) to determine where the line or plane crosses the S axis, which equals the log of "a." One can then determine the value of "a" by consulting a logarithmic table.

If this is done with the Auerbach data, then $b_1 = .30$, $b_2 = -.31$, and $a = 14$. This means that the exponential equation can now be read as $S = 14 \cdot \$L^{.30} \cdot \$C^{-31}$. Because a number taken to a negative exponent means the same as the reciprocal of the number taken to the same exponent made positive, and since a decimal exponent close to .33 is the same as the cube root of the number to which the exponent is taken, this exponential equation simplifies to $S = 14 \cdot \sqrt[3]{\$L} / \sqrt[3]{\$C}$.

Note that in this equation as $\$L$ gets bigger, S gets bigger; and as $\$C$ gets bigger, S gets smaller (just as in the constraint 10 linear equation). One should also note that the above exponential equation fits the Auerbach data better than the linear regression equation in constraint 10 in view of the fact that the sum of the squared deviations from the dots to the exponential line is slightly less than the sum of the squared deviations to the linear regression line.[35]

In order to better understand the problem involved in minimizing total costs and maximizing total benefits when dealing with a diminishing returns satisfaction curve, it is helpful to graph one or more satisfaction curves and one or more total cost lines. For the cost minimization problem, the most relevant satisfaction curve is the minimum satisfaction one. It is, however, difficult to draw a curve accurately because so many points must be determined, whereas the position of a straight line can be determined simply by finding two accurate points and then connecting them. Fortunately, an exponential curve can be easily and meaningfully converted to a straight line by finding two accurate points for the curve on logarithmic-interval (rather than equal-interval) graph paper and connecting these two points.

Figure 2 graphs on logarithmic paper the diminishing returns satisfaction line for a minimum satisfaction level of 7.00. If one expresses $\$L$ in terms of $\$C$ in the simplified exponential equation, then $\$L = (7.00 \cdot \sqrt[3]{\$C} / 14)^3$ which easily reduces to $\$L = \$C/8$, or $\$C = 8 \cdot \$L$. Therefore, to draw the minimum satisfaction line, one can simply connect the point that corresponds to $\$L = 1$, $\$C = 8$ and the point that corresponds to $\$L = 12$, $\$C = 96$. In a similar manner, the maximum satisfaction line can be drawn where $S = 12.00$. It is even easier to draw the maximum and minimum $\$L$ and $\$C$ lines since they are unaffected by the fact that logarithmic paper is being used, although there is a change in the physical distances between those maximums and minimums from Figure 1.

The minimum and maximum total cost lines which would be straight on equal-interval paper now become curves on log-interval paper. As before, any point on a total cost line involves the same total cost as any other point on the same line, just as any point on a benefit line involves the same total benefit as any other point on the same line. Plotting the minimum total cost line therefore simply involves plotting and connecting a number of points each one of which has a value for $L and $C such that the sum of those two values adds up to $61.50 or up to $68.34 for the maximum total cost line.

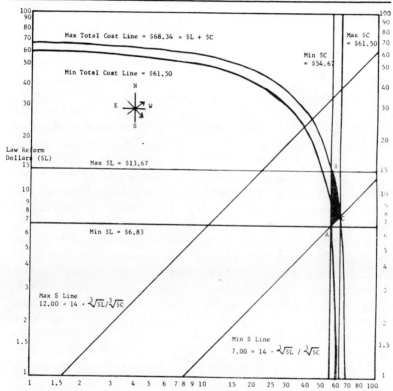

Point A is where total cost is minimized while providing at least 7.00 units of satisfaction.
$L = $6.83. $C = $54.67. TC = $61.50. S = 7.02.

Point B is where satisfaction is maximized while not spending more than $68.34.
$L = $13.67. $C = $54.67. TC = $68.34. S = 8.83.

Figure 2: Allocating $L and $C to Minimize Costs or Maximize Benefits (with diminishing returns and a positively-sloped equal-benefit line)

GOALS TO OPTIMIZE

One can see from Figure 2 that point A is the point where total costs are minimized while still providing the minimum 7.00 satisfaction level, because that is the point within the shaded feasible region where all the constraints are simultaneously met which is farthest away from the maximum cost line and closest to the minimum cost line. To determine exactly where point A is and the value of $L and $C at that point, one must decide what lines or equations logically intersect at the point where total costs are minimized and where at least minimum satisfaction is obtained. This intersection is the point where the minimum $C line intersects the minimum satisfaction line, provided that intersection does not occur below the minimum $L line. It is wasteful to spend more than the minimum $C in view of the fact that $C correlates negatively with satisfaction, and thus extra spending on $C means reduced satisfaction.

To find optimum $L, plug minimum $C which is $54.67 into the minimum S formula, $7.00 = 14 \cdot \sqrt[3]{\$L} / \sqrt[3]{\$C}$, and solve for $L. Doing so, however, will yield an $L of $6.80 which is less than the minimum $L. This means the optimum $L has to be the minimum $L of $6.83 in order to satisfy the minimum $L constraint, even though an $L of $6.83 combined with a $C or $54.67 will produce an S of 7.02 which is higher than the minimum S of 7.00 but still satisfies the minimum S constraint.[36]

In comparing the Figure 2 cost minimization solution with the one from Figure 1, it should be noted that the optimum total cost in Figure 2 is only $61.50, a savings of $6.84 per participant. This is even more than the savings of $6.59 per participant in Figure 1, and thus even more than the estimated $6,000,000 national annual savings for the OEO Legal Services Program. As with Figure 1, having a minimum $C as high as $54.67 produces a binding constraint and thereby creates opportunity costs and lost savings. Unlike Figure 1, having a minimum $L as high as $6.83 is also a binding constraint because less $L could still produce the minimum 7.00 S without changing the minimum $C.

It may be partly a coincidence of the example used that the diminishing returns solution for optimum $L and $C came out as close to the constant returns solution as it did since one might expect a greater difference. The similarity between the two solutions indicates that diminishing returns are not so great in the expenditure of dollars for law reform and case handling relative to the satisfaction obtained, at least within the range of expenditures that are currently being made. This may further indicate that substantial additional sums can be spent on legal services without soon incurring diminishing returns.

Point B is the point in Figure 2 where benefits are maximized for the average agency below the $68.34 per participant limit. This is the benefit maximization point because it is the point within the shaded feasible region where all the constraints are simultaneously met which is farthest away from the minimum satisfaction line and closest to the maximum satisfaction line. As with Figure 1, point B is logically the point where the minimum $C of $54.67 is spent and the maximum $L of $13.67. At that point, the total cost will be the maximum cost of $68.34. To calculate the satisfaction level at that point, simply plug the optimum $L and $C into the formula $S = .14 \cdot \sqrt[3]{\$L} / \sqrt[3]{\$C}$ and solve for S. Doing so yields an S of 8.83.

In comparing the Figure 2 benefit maximization solution with the one for Figure 1, it should be noted that the optimum total satisfaction in Figure 1 is 9.27 as contrasted to 8.83 in Figure 2. Both represent substantial percentage gains over the 6.45 satisfaction rating which the average agency had in the Auerbach data. To the extent that the diminishing returns relation more accurately fits the empirical data, the gain from 6.45 to 8.83 or 37 percent is the more realistic gain available by better allocation to $L and $C while still only spending $68.34 per participant. As with Figure 1, both the minimum $C constraint and the maximum $L constraint are preventing point B from rising higher toward the maximum satisfaction level, and they are thus creating opportunity costs which may or may not be politically justifiable.

Point C in Figure 2 (like Figure 1) is the irrational point where costs are maximized at the minimum satisfaction level and where benefits are minimized at the maximum cost level. As with Figure 1, a compromise position can be arrived at between point A and point B wherein one can choose a midpoint $L of $10.25 which means a $C of $54.67, TC of $64.92, and S of 8.01. Rather than interpolate to determine the compromise value of S, one can obtain greater accuracy by plugging the compromise values of $L and $C into the formula for relating S to $L and $C.

One important comparison between the Figure 2 approach and the Figure 1 approach is that all the cost minimization and benefit maximization (once the constraints have been determined) can be done for Figure 1 by easy to use canned computer programs. The Figure 2 curved line diminishing returns approach, however, generally requires graphing to arrive at approximate solutions, or the use of a desk calculator to arrive at exact solutions, since computer programs are not so available for handling optimizing problems with nonlinear constraints.

IV. CHOOSING AMONG LEGAL SERVICES ACTIVITIES WITH DIMINISHING RETURNS AND A NEGATIVELY SLOPED EQUAL BENEFIT LINE

CONSTRAINTS TO SATISFY

Although Figure 2 complies with the empirical data gathered by both Auerbach and Kettelle, it is unusual to have benefit lines that are positively sloped from southeast to northwest rather than inversely sloped from northeast to southwest. In other words, it is more common for Activity 1 dollars and Activity 2 dollars to move in opposite directions in order to hold total benefits constant than for them to move in the same direction. A positively sloped equal benefit line has no effect on the procedures used in linear programming where all the relations are straight lines. Such a line, however, does affect the appropriate methodology for optimizing costs or benefits when diminishing returns are involved.

In order to demonstrate how one minimizes costs and maximizes benefits with a diminishing returns equal benefit line that is negatively sloped, as is more commonly the case, let us assume the constraint 10 relation is $S = .7 \cdot \sqrt[3]{\$L} \cdot \sqrt[3]{\$C}$, rather than $S = 14 \cdot \sqrt[3]{\$L} / \sqrt[3]{\$C}$. By changing the division sign to a multiplication sign, the relation between \$C and S is changed from negative to positive, and the relation between \$C and \$L is changed from positive to negative. By changing the value of "a" from 14 to .7, we create a minimum satisfaction line that falls between the minimum and maximum total cost lines. Figure 3 shows the minimum and maximum satisfaction lines corresponding to this new equal benefit equation.

To illustrate how to minimize costs at a minimum level of satisfaction or maximize satisfaction at a maximum level of costs using the total cost and total benefit lines of Figure 3, it is necessary to ignore the minimum and maximum \$L and \$C constraint lines. This is so because if those lines are complied with, then there is no point on the minimum satisfaction line that is simultaneously between the minimum and maximum \$L lines and the minimum and maximum \$C lines. Let us make the reasonable assumption that the minimum \$L is zero dollars, and the maximum \$L is \$68.34, and that likewise the minimum \$C is zero dollars, and the maximum \$C is \$68.34. In other words, let us remove the minimum and maximum constraints on the separate activity variables as is often done in linear programming problems and see what happens. One obvious result is that the new feasible region is the shaded area between the minimum satisfaction line and the maximum total cost line. What is not so obvious is

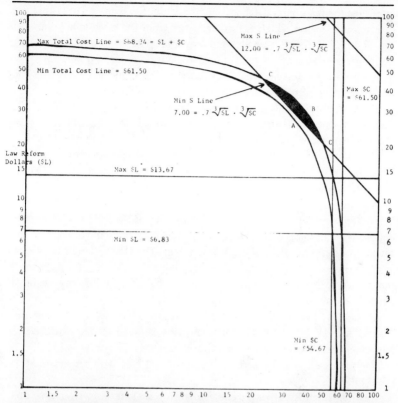

Point A is where total cost is minimized while providing at least 7.00 units of satisfaction.
$L = $31.62. $C = $31.62. TC = $63.24. S = 7.00.

Point B is where satisfaction is maximized while not spending more than $68.34.
$L = $34.17. $C = $34.17. TC = $68.34. S = 7.37.

Figure 3: Allocating $L and $C to Minimize Costs or Maximize Benefits (with diminishing returns and a negatively-sloped equal-benefit line)

exactly what point within that shaded area is the optimum minimum cost point for allocating $L and $C, and what point is the optimum maximum benefit point.

GOALS TO OPTIMIZE

The cost minimization point is at point A. Geometrically, this corresponds to a point on the minimum satisfaction line that is about midway between the two points where the minimum satisfaction line intersects the maximum total cost line, because that is the point within the new feasible region which is farthest away from the maximum total cost line and closest to the former minimum total cost line. Actually, there is no longer a minimum total cost line if there is no longer a minimum $L or minimum $C; therefore, what was formerly the minimum total cost line should be referred to as an equal cost line equal to $61.50.

To determine exactly where point A is and the value of $L and $C at that point, one must first state $L in terms of $C in the latest version of the combined constraint 8 and 10 formula which is $7.00 = .7 \cdot \sqrt[3]{\$L} \cdot \sqrt[3]{\$C}$. This means $\$L = [7.00 / (.7 \cdot \sqrt[3]{\$C})]^3$ which simplifies down to $\$L = 1000 / \$C$. If we know that total cost = $L + $C, then we also know that total cost = $(1000/\$C) + \$C$.

We must next find the calculus derivative of the total cost with respect to $C for the equation total cost = $(1000/\$C) + \$C$. The derivative of Y (a dependent variable) with respect to X (an independent variable) is the number corresponding to the ratio between a change in Y and a change in X when the value of the change in X becomes so small as to approach zero, but not quite reach it. A derivative can also be thought of as the algebraic expression for the slope of the tangent to a curve at any given point on the curve such as the point where the curve is at a minimum or maximum. Fortunately, tables are available whereby one can read off the derivative of any expression without fully understanding what a derivative is.[37] Such a table indicates that the derivative of the total cost with respect to $C is $(-1000/\$C^2) + 1$.

We then set this derivative equal to zero which means we are now at a point where there is no slope, or a horizontal slope, between total costs and $C, and total costs are thus at a minimum at the 7.00 given level of satisfaction. We then solve for $C at this point. If $(-1000/\$C^2) + 1 = 0$, then C = $31.62. For the final step, we plug this value of $C into the equation $7.00 = .7 \sqrt[3]{\$L} \cdot \sqrt[3]{\$C}$ and solve for $L. Doing so reveals that the optimum $L is also $31.62.[38] Thus, at point A, the total cost is $63.24 with a satisfaction level of 7.00.

In effect, what we have done through the above use of differential calculus is to find the value of $L and $C at the point where the lowest possible total cost line just barely touches the minimum satisfaction line. This lowest total cost line has a value of $63.24 at any point along the line. A total cost line one penny less than $63.24 (if the arithmetic is done accurately) would not quite touch up to or be tangent to the minimum S line, and thus would produce less than 7.00 satisfaction units. Likewise, a total cost line one penny more than $63.24 would intersect the minimum S line rather than just barely touch it, and thus would produce more than 7.00 satisfaction units.[39]

Note that the optimum solution involved spending some money for law reform and some money for case handling even though there was no minimum $L and no minimum $C, and thus, in terms of the constraints, all of the money could have been spent for $L. One reason some money was spent for $L and some for $C is that, in setting up the hypothetical constraint 10 which would show a negatively sloping equal benefit line, we gave $L and $C equal weight in determining S since the cube root is taken of both $L and $C in the formula. Doing so not only causes some $L and some $C to be spent in the optimum solution, but also causes equal amounts to be spent on $L and $C. However, even if the weight given to $L were substantially greater (as would be that obtained by taking only the square root of $L in constraint 10), some money would probably be spent on $C in the optimum solution, because although at lower expenditure levels it would be more efficient to spend on $L, the phenomenon of diminishing returns would cause continued spending on $L to become inefficient relative to spending on $C. This point of inefficiency might be reached before enough money could be spent on $L to produce a 7.00 minimum satisfaction level.

The only binding constraint in this cost minimization situation is the minimum satisfaction line. If it were lowered, additional savings could be had and opportunity costs avoided. As before, however, we cannot judge whether lowering the minimum S line would be worth the dollars saved without knowing how many dollars one satisfaction unit is worth. With a minimum S line of 7.00, there is a savings of $5.10 from the $68.34 available per participant. This savings, however, is as hypothetical as the slope and shape of the minimum benefit line.

The benefit maximization point is at point B. Geometrically, this corresponds to a point on the maximum total cost line that is about midway between the two points where the minimum satisfaction line intersects the maximum total cost line, because that is the point within the feasible region farthest away from the minimum S line of 7.00 and closest to the maximum S line of 12.00.

To determine exactly where point B is and the value of $L and $C at that point, one must first state $L in terms of $C in the combined constraint 6 and 7 formula which is $68.34 = $L + $C. This means $L = $68.34 − $C. If we know that satisfaction units obtained = $.7 \cdot \sqrt[3]{\$L}$ $\cdot \sqrt[3]{\$C}$, then we also know that satisfaction = $.7 \cdot \sqrt[3]{\$68.34 - \$C} \cdot \sqrt[3]{\$C}$. We must next find the calculus derivative of satisfaction (as the dependent variable) with respect to $C (as the independent variable) for the equation $S = .7 \cdot \sqrt[3]{\$68.34 - \$C} \cdot \sqrt[3]{\$C}$. By consulting a table of derivatives as we did with the cost minimization problem, we find that the value of the simplified derivative of S with respect to $C is $(-.462 \cdot \$C + \$15.78654) /$ $[\$C^{.67} \cdot (\$68.34 - \$C)^{.67}]$. We next set this derivative or slope equal to zero to be at the point where S is a maximum at a total cost of $68.34. We then solve for $C in this equation. Doing so reveals that optimum $C = $-15.78654/-.462 = \$34.17$. For the final step, we plug this value of $C into the equation $68.34 = $L + $C and solve for $L. Doing so reveals that the optimum $L is also $34.17.[40]

To determine the satisfaction level at this point, we plug the above benefit maximization values of $L and $C into the formula $S = .7 \cdot \sqrt[3]{\$L} \cdot \sqrt[3]{\$C}$, and we find that S = 7.37. Considering that the average S for the 49 agencies in the Auerbach data was only 6.45 with an average total cost of $68.34, this means that by properly allocating our total cost available to $L and $C, we can obtain an increase of .92 satisfaction units or 14 percent if the above satisfaction formula were real rather than hypothetical. The only binding constraint in this benefit maximization situation is the maximum total cost line. If it were raised, additional benefits could be had and opportunity costs avoided, but we do not know whether those additional satisfaction units would be worth the additional dollars.

In effect, what we have done through the above use of differential calculus is to find the value of $L and $C at the point where the highest possible satisfaction line just barely touches, or is tangent to, the maximum total cost line. As previously mentioned, this highest possible S line has a value of 7.37 at any point along the line. A satisfaction line .01 more than 7.37 (if the arithmetic is done accurately) would be beyond the capacity of a maximum total cost of $68.34 to reach. Likewise, a satisfaction line .01 unit less than 7.37 would be needlessly below the capacity of a maximum total cost of $68.34.[41]

One might question the need for finding a derivative, setting it equal to zero, and solving for $C (as we just did) when in this example one could have found that $C = $34.17 by merely dividing the $68.34 maximum cost by 2. This, however, is only true for this example because $L and $C are given the same cube root weights in the formula relating total benefits to $L and $C. In a less simple but more realistic example, $L and $C would have different weights, and the exact optimum $L and $C for maximizing benefits on the maximum total cost line in Figure 3 could be derived only by consulting a table of derivatives and doing the algebra and arithmetic involved. One could, however, arrive at approximate optimums for $L and $C simply by observing where B seems to fall on a graph like Figure 3.

If spending the maximum total cost results in achieving more than the maximum total possible satisfaction, then find the value of $L and $C at the point where total costs are minimized at the 12.00 rather than 7.00 level of satisfaction. This involves going through the same steps described earlier for finding the value of $L and $C at a cost minimization point by finding the derivative of the total cost with respect to $C for the equation total cost = (5038/$C) + $C, setting this derivative equal to zero, solving for optimum $C, and then plugging that value back into the equation $12.00 = .7 \cdot \sqrt[3]{\$L} \cdot \sqrt[3]{\$C}$ to solve for optimum $L.

As mentioned in discussing optimization involving diminishing returns and a positively sloped equal benefit line, canned computer programs are not available for handling optimizing problems with nonlinear constraints. This is likewise so with diminishing returns and negatively sloped equal benefit lines. A desk calculator, however, can greatly facilitate the calculus arithmetic involved. If more than two activity or independent variables are present, one can, in effect, group the activity variables into conflicting groups by the calculus approach of partial differentiation or partial derivatives (Baumol, 1965: 57-59; Richmond, 1968: 78-79).

The two point C's in Figure 3 (like point C in Figure 1 and Figure 2) represent the irrational positions where costs are maximized at the minimum satisfaction level and where benefits are minimized at the maximum cost level. With the data from Figure 3, and compromise optimum between points A and B is $L = $32.90 per participant, $C = $32.90, TC = $65.80, and S = 7.19. By this stage in the development of the minimization and maximization methodology as applied to the Legal Services Program, one should be able to see that optimum points A, B, and C, as well as the ten constraints, are all present in one form or another in Figures 1, 2, and 3 as explained in the accompanying text.

V. SOME CONCLUSIONS

The most important *methodological* principles developed in more detail in this analysis are five in number. These principles all relate to how one can make better policy decisions by allocating scarce financial resources in order to obtain more for one's money.

First, in choosing between alternative activities or deciding how much to spend on each activity, it is helpful to both algebraically and geometrically determine (1) the minimum and maximum level desired for each activity, for total costs, and for total benefits, and (2) the relation between expenditure for each activity on the one hand and total costs and total benefits on the other hand.

Second, in determining the relation between the activities and the total benefits, it is helpful to gather data on specific instances of activity spending and benefits obtained and to feed this data into a canned computer program in order to obtain the coefficients for a linear or logarithmic regression line.

Third, in order to minimize total costs, find a point geometrically or algebraically representing the expenditure values for each activity which is farthest down from the maximum cost level but provides at least the minimum satisfaction level.

Fourth, in order to maximize total benefits, find a point representing the expenditure values for each activity that is farthest up from the minimum satisfaction level, but does not exceed the maximum cost level.

Fifth, seek to maximize benefits minus costs if both benefits and costs can be measured in terms of the same units. Otherwise, choose between cost minimization or benefit maximization on the basis of one's values or the values of some controlling group, or else compromise between cost minimization and benefit maximization.

The most important *substantive* principles developed in more detail in this analysis are four in number. These principles all relate to how the OEO Legal Services Program can allocate its scarce resources in order to obtain more for its money.

First, substantial reductions in total costs expended by the OEO Legal Services Program seem possible if linear or other optimizing programming techniques are used to more rationally allocate local agency budgets between law reform and case handling, without resulting in lowering the satisfaction level below the minimum desired and especially without resulting in lowering the satisfaction level below the currently prevailing low level.[42]

Second, substantial increases in satisfaction by the OEO Legal Services Program seem possible if linear or other optimizing programming techniques are used to more rationally allocate agency budgets between law reform and case handling, without raising currently prevailing agency budget levels.

Third, a dollar spent for law reform tends to produce substantially more satisfaction than a dollar spent for case handling. In fact, a dollar spent for case handling produces negative satisfaction at least to the extent it detracts from law reform dollars available.

Fourth, substantially more dollars can be spent on the OEO Legal Services Program before extra dollars produce significantly diminishing incremental returns.

The real value of all this analysis, however, is not in laying out a set of abstract principles as a kind of mathematical recreation. Nor is it to make the Legal Services Program more efficient. Instead, the real or broader value lies in the possibility that the general principles described here with a Legal Services application will be expanded by other researchers and used by policy makers and policy appliers in more efficiently allocating scarce governmental resources in a large variety of legal policy situations.[43]

NOTES

1. One exception is Laidlaw (1972).

2. For a review of the literature of scientific legal-policy decision making, see Mayo and Jones (1964). Some more recent related material is included in Tullock (1971).

3. The Jarmel (1972) and Semmel (1970) readings include excerpts from Gary Bellow, Edgar Cahn, Geoffrey Hazard, and others. For over 1,000 bibliographic items on legal services (most with long abstracts), see Chilton Research Services (1971).

4. According to the Kettelle report (1971), the on-site visits were conducted by teams typically composed of an attorney acting as team leader, two additional attorneys, and one community analyst. Criteria used in the selection of attorney members included empathy with the needs of the poor community and an understanding of and appreciation for the goals of the Office of Legal Services.

5. ,The quantity of law reform and related activities is given in three verbal categories in the Auerbach data rather than as a percentage, although it is given as a percentage in the Kettelle data. The first verbal category in the Auerbach data is "virtually no other activity [other than case handling]"; the second category is "some special activities in law reform and group representation"; and the third category is "considerable amount of other [than] case activity." These three verbal categories were translated to 2 percent, 10 percent, and 20 percent, respectively, on the basis of observing that in the Kettelle data the average of the bottom third of the projects was about 2 percent, the middle third about 10 percent, and the top third about 20 percent. The translations also make sense in light of the commonsense meaning of the verbalization used and statements made in the allocation-debate literature.

6. The number of dollars per participant was used rather than the raw number of dollars so as to provide comparability between agencies operating with different clientele sizes. The number of dollars per population within the geographical area of each agency would not be as accurate because two geographical areas of equal size may differ in the number of poor people and especially in the number of poor people who participate in the legal services program. Counting clients or counting cases produces approximately the same results in the optimizing solutions since agencies tend to rank the same on quantity of clients or cases. Some clients or participants have multiple cases, but some cases have multiple clients. Agencies do have more participants than cases, even if the word participants is used to refer only to immediate recipients of services and not to those benefiting indirectly.

7. A rating of 1 through 3 means: "Project has critical deficiencies. Close down

or cut back project." A rating of 4 through 6 means: "Project has internal problems. Requires technical assistance. Fund at project-in-place level." A 7 through 9 means: "Project operating efficiently. Could benefit from technical assistance. Fund at project-in-place level." A 10 through 12 means: "Project operating efficiently. A strong force in the War on Poverty. Expand if project can effectively handle additional resources."

8. The Kettelle data provides direct percentages on percent of law reform rather than percentages translated from verbal categories, and the Kettelle data provides the number of project participants rather than the number of planned project participants. The other variables are measured the same in both sets of data. Copies of the Kettelle final report, which contain the raw data, are available from the Evaluation Division of the Office of Economic Opportunity or from the National Technical Information Services of the U.S. Department of Commerce. The Auerbach data is only available on computer tapes for special research from the OEO Office of Legal Services.

9. The especially deviant cases were also removed from the analysis because they have a tendency to distort the degree and even the direction of the relationship between (1) case handling and law reform dollars spent and (2) satisfaction obtained.

10. In the evaluation questionnaires, law reform and related activities (as contrasted to individual service cases) refer to (1) law reform (i.e., amending existing laws or changing regulations and practices thereby benefiting others in addition to individual client); (2) economic development (includes technical assistance such as forming cooperatives, negotiating loans, small business counseling, and acting as a promoter, incorporator, and advisor to entrepreneurs); (3) community education (i.e., informing target community members of what the law can do for them); and (4) group representation. See Kettelle Corporation (1971: 132-133).

11. One of the sixteen agencies was eliminated from the analysis of the Kettelle data. Without that deviant agency, the Kettelle agencies spent a total amount of $47.50 per participant, $39.22 (or 83 percent) on case handling, and $8.28 (or 17 percent) on law reform. The one deviant case spent a total amount of $270.08 per participant.

12. Policy-making problems that do not involve the allocation of scarce resources to two or more activities include such controversial issues as whether to pass legislation abolishing capital punishment, legalizing marijuana, prohibiting malapportioned legislatures, or legalizing medical abortions. For a generalized model for handling such policy problems, see Nagel (1969: 360-373).

13. As indicated in note 9, there are only three categories in which the agencies are placed with regard to percent of effort devoted to law reform activities corresponding to 2 percent, 10 percent, and 20 percent. The verbal description of the 2 percent category as being "virtually no other activity [other than case handling]," and the general rejection in the debate literature of so low a level of law reform indicate that legal services agencies should seek to reach at least the next higher category.

14. The maximum allowable $L in working with the Kettelle data was considered to be 40 percent of the average budget rather than 20 percent as with the Auerbach data because (1) some of the existing agencies in the Kettelle data had indicated an average percent of attorney time on law reform at 35 and 36 percent, and (2) doing so allows for a broader range in which the optimum allocation of $L and $C can be positioned.

15. Instead of stating law reform and case handling in terms of monetary units, one could have stated those activities in terms of man hours spent. Information on dollars rather than hours, however, is more readily available. Dollars are also interchangeable, but hours of senior, more experienced lawyers are not generally interchangeable with hours of junior lawyers.

16. See note 6.

17. For additional detail on constructing a linear regression line to relate two variables, see Blalock (1960: 273-285, 326-329) and Guilford (1956: 365-369, 390-396). The reason law reform related activities and case handling are the only two independent variables used is because we are trying to decide an optimum balance to allocate to these two types of activities. For a discussion of other variables related to evaluator satisfaction (such as the nature of the agency personnel, the local bar, the poverty community, and the geographical region), see Champagne (1973).

18. The correlation coefficient between $L and S is +.64, whereas the correlation coefficient between $C and S is −.27.

19. In the Auerbach data there is a +.26 correlation between $C and $L. This means that when $C is high, $L also tends to be high and vice versa, but not necessarily as a causal relation. More likely $C and $L are both co-effects of how high the overall budget is. If the overall budget is held constant, then by definition additional case handling means a reduction in law reform since TC = $C + $L.

20. If budget amounts and satisfaction scores for each agency could be obtained over time, a linear programming routine could be applied to allocating funds among the approximately 300 legal services agencies so as to maximize national satisfaction from the program.

21. In the Kettelle data, the correlation between satisfaction and $C was positive when $L was ignored. However, when $L was held constant, $C had a negative weight in the regression equation. This means that among agencies that are approximately alike on $L, those that are high on $C have a lower S than those that are low on $C.

22. The ten constraints for the Kettelle data calculated by methods similar to those used for the Auerbach data are as follows:

(1) Minimum $L = $4.74 or 10 percent of maximum total cost.
(2) Maximum $L = $19.00 or 40 percent of maximum total cost. (See note 17.)
(3) Minimum $C = $28.50 or 60 percent of maximum total cost.
(4) Maximum $C = $42.75 or 90 percent of maximum total cost.
(5) Minimum total cost = $33.24.
(6) Maximum total cost = $47.50.
(7) Total cost = $L + $C.
(8) Minimum benefits = 7.00.
(9) Maximum benefits = 12.00.
(10) Total benefits = 7.16 + (.42 · $L) − (.06 · $C).

23. For the Kettelle data, the cost minimization point (corresponding to the Kettelle constraints in note 22) is $L = $4.75, $C = $28.50, total cost = $33.25, and S = 7.38. In this example, the minimum $L and the minimum $C turn out to be the optimum $L and optimum $C because by spending the minimum of each, one can obtain more than the 7.00 minimum satisfaction level.

24. To be exact, if one plugs a value for $L of $6.83 and a value for $C of $54.67 into the formula S = 6.29 + (.34 · $L) − (.03 · $C), then the value of S comes out to be only 6.97. The value of S by spending at the minimum total cost line would be

substantially less than 7.00 if the minimum satisfaction line would have had either a steeper slope or would have begun at a point to the left of Figure 1 farther away from the minimum $L line. The difference between 6.97 and 7.00 is .03 satisfaction units, not .03 dollars. One satisfaction unit may be worth many dollars.

25. There were 265 legal services projects as of January, 1969 (Law in Action, 1969a: 4). The budget for 1970 was $58,000,000 (Law in Action, 1969b: 5). Figures giving the number of legal services agencies at a given point in time vary depending on whether one counts the separate community agencies for multiple-community programs like the California Rural Legal Assistance or the downstate Illinois Land of Lincoln Legal Assistance Foundation.

26. If the total budget available per participant is higher than $71.00, then even by spending only the minimum 10 percent on $L, a satisfaction level greater than 7.00 will be obtained. This $71 figure was arrived at by solving for B in the equation $7.00 = 6.29 + (.34 \cdot .1B) - (.03 \cdot .8B)$.

27. If the total budget available per participant is as low as $16.14, then by spending the maximum 20 percent of $L, a satisfaction level of 7.00 can still be obtained (but not if the budget is lower than $16.14). This figure was arrived at by solving for B in the equation $7.00 = 6.29 + (.34 \cdot .2B) - (.03 \cdot .8B)$.

28. For additional detail on cost minimization and production economics, see Samuelson (1967: 523–529) and Baumol (1965: 250-294).

29. For the Kettelle data, the benefit maximization point (corresponding to the Kettelle constraints in note 22) is $L = $15.73, $C = $28.50, total cost = $44.23, and S = 12.00. In this example, the maximum S level of 12.00 can be obtained without spending the total budget of $47.50. Instead, the minimum $C is spent and just enough $L above the minimum $L to bring S up to the 12.00 maximum.

30. If the total budget available per participant is $129.77, then exactly 12.00 units of satisfaction can be obtained by spending the maximum 20 percent on $L. This $129.77 figure was arrived at by solving for B in the equation $12.00 = 6.29 + (.34 \cdot .2B) - (.03 \cdot .8B)$. Therefore, with a budget larger than $129.77, less than 20 percent should be spent on $L or else some of the $L will be wasted seeking theoretically nonexistent additional satisfaction. If, however, the total budget available per participant is higher than $571.00, then even spending the minimum 10 percent on $L will still result in exceeding the 12.00 maximum satisfaction level. This $571 figure was arrived at by solving for B in the equation $12.00 = 6.29 + (.34 \cdot .1B) - (.03 \cdot .8B)$.

31. For additional detail on cost minimization and consumption economics, see Samuelson (1967: 429-434) and Baumol (1965: 169-249).

32. On the measurement of nonmonetary costs and benefits, see Black (1968: 37-89), Dorfman (1964), and Guilford (1954: 154-301).

33. One cannot translate satisfaction units into dollars by determining the slope of the regression line between satisfaction obtained and total cost spent for each of the 49 Auerbach data agencies, because such a line would represent the relation between quantity of legal service satisfaction units *supplied* and the price per unit, rather than the relation between the quantity of legal service satisfaction units *demanded* and the price per unit. A supply curve has a positive or direct relation between units supplied and the price paid, whereas a demand curve has a negative or inverse relation between units demanded and the price paid. These two curves or lines may also have different shapes as well as directions. This problem is basically one of identifying the proper equation in a simultaneous relationship. See Baumol (1965: 221-228) and Blalock (1969: 48-59).

34. For further detail on exponents and logarithms, see Baumol (1965: 17-19), or any intermediate algebra text.

35. Stated in other terms, the multiple correlation is .84 between Log \$L and Log \$C as independent variables and Log S as the dependent variable, whereas the multiple correlation is only .64 between \$L and \$C as independent variables and S as the dependent variable.

36. Actually, the S level at point A in Figure 2 is 7.15 if one does not round off the original b_1 and b_2 from .31 and $-.31$, respectively, to .33, and if one does not round off the original "a" value from 13.9 to 14.

37. Virtually everything you always wanted to know about calculus applied to minimization and maximization problems but may have been afraid to ask can be found in Baumol (1965: 42-69), Richmond (1968: 40-66, 577), and Blalock (1969: 166-171).

38. If one finds the derivative of total cost with respect to one input variable in the diminishing returns relation using only algebraic symbols rather than numbers, then the optimum value of the input variable at minimum total costs equals b_2/b_1 times MIN S/"a" where b_2/b_1 is raised to the power of $b_1/(b_2 + b_1)$ and where the second element is raised to the power of $1(b_1 b_2)$. If one considers \$C to be the input variable, substituting $1/3$ for b_1, $1/3$ for b_2, 7.00 for minimum satisfaction, and .7 for "a" yields an optimum \$C of \$31.62.

39. In light of the above tangential-curves conceptualization, as an alternative to finding the derivative of the total cost with respect to \$C or \$L, one could find: (1) the derivative or slope of \$C with respect to \$L in light of the fact that \$C = TC $-$ \$L, and (2) the derivative or slope of \$C with respect to \$L in light of the fact that $\$C = [7.00 / (.7 \cdot \sqrt[3]{\$L})]^3 = 1000 \cdot \$L^{-1}$ when S equals 7.00. The first derivative equals -1, and the second derivative equals $-1000 / \$L^2$. If these two derivatives are set equal to each other (to show we are looking for the value of \$L at the point of minimum TC where the slopes of the two curves are equal or tangential), then $-1 = -1000 / \$L^2$, and \$L = \$31.62. Plugging this value of \$L into the second equation above yields a value of \$31.62 for \$C. The value of \$C could also be found by setting the derivative of \$L with respect to \$C (where \$L = TC $-$ \$C) equal to the derivative of \$L with respect to \$C (where \$L = 1000 / \$C), and then solving for \$C.

40. If one finds the derivative of total satisfaction with respect to one input variable in the diminishing returns relation using only algebraic symbols rather than numbers, then the optimum value of the input variable at maximum satisfaction equals b_2 times $1/b_1$ times the value of the other input variable raised to a power equal to $2b_1 - 1$ with the product resulting from multiplying those three terms together raised to a power equal to $1/(2b_2 - 1)$. This equation formula thus gives us the ratio of optimum \$C to optimum \$L (or other pair of input variables) for any regression values. For example, if $b_1 = 1/3$, and $b_2 = 1/3$, then \$C = \$L. Further since \$L = TC $-$ \$C, then \$C = TC/2 = \$34.17.

41. In light of the above tangential-curves conceptualization, as an alternative to finding the derivative of the total satisfaction with respect to \$C or \$L, one could find (1) the derivative or slope of \$C with respect to \$L in light of the fact that \$C = \$68.34 $-$ \$L, and (2) the derivative or slope of \$C with respect to \$L in light of the fact that $\$C = [S/(.7 \cdot \sqrt[3]{\$L})]^3 = 2.915 \, S^3 \cdot \$L^{-1}$. If these two derivatives are set equal to each other (to show we are looking for the value of \$L at the point of maximum S where the slopes of the two curves are equal or tangential), then $-1 = -2.915 \, S^3/\$L^2$, and thus $\$L = \sqrt[2]{2.915 \, S^3}$. By substituting $.7 \cdot \sqrt[3]{\$L} \cdot \sqrt[3]{\$C}$ for

the value of S in this last equation, we find that $L = 1.00 \cdot C$. This means $L = \$68.34 - \$L$ or $L = \$34.17$, and $C = \$34.17$. The value of C could also be found by setting the derivative of L with respect to C (where $L = \$68.34 - \$C$) equal to the derivative of L with respect to C (where $L = 2.915\, S^3/\$C$), and then solving for C.

42. "Low" level refers to the fact that the average agency now produces only 6.45 units of satisfaction, but the minimum desired is 7.00 since any agency below that level was considered by the evaluators to be a "project that has internal problems and requires technical assistance," whereas a project at that 7.00 level was considered to be a "project operating efficiently."

43. Some controversial issues involving the allocation of scarce governmental resources include allocating funds (1) between busing versus compensatory education in improving educational opportunities for poor children, (2) between subsidizing low-rent public housing versus home ownership for the poor and lower middle class, (3) between anti-water-pollution enforcement programs versus water clean-up facilities, (4) between fair employment enforcement activities versus manpower training to provide better employment opportunities to minorities, (5) between urban and rural legal services agencies, and (6) among the approximately 300 legal services agencies so as to maximize national satisfaction from the program.

REFERENCES

AGNEW, S. (1972) "What's wrong with the Legal Services Program." American Bar Association Journal 58 (September): 930-932.

Auerbach Corporation (1971) Office of Legal Services Individual Project Evaluations Final Report. Washington, D.C.: OEO Office of Legal Services.

BALDWIN, F. (1972) Evaluating the OEO Legal Services Program. Washington, D.C.: OEO Evaluation Division.

BAUMOL, W. (1965) Economic Theory and Operations Analysis. Englewood Cliffs, N.J.: Prentice Hall.

BLACK, G. (1968) The Application of Systems Analysis to Government Operations. New York: Praeger.

BLALOCK, H. (1969) Theory Construction: From Verbal to Mathematical Formulations. Englewood CLiffs, N.J.: Prentice Hall.

——— (1960) Social Statistics. New York: McGraw Hill.

Catholic Lawyer (1968) "The O.E.O. and legal services: a symposium." Volume 14 (Spring): 91-174.

CHAMPAGNE, A. (1973) "Legal services: a study of program implementation at the local level." Ph.D. dissertation. Urbana: University of Illinois.

Chilton Research Services (1971) Legal Services Evaluation Study Literature Search Report. Washington, D.C.: Department of Commerce National Technical Information Service.

DORFMAN, R. (1964) Measuring Benefits in Government Investments. Washington, D.C.: Brookings Institution.

DUFFY, H. et al. (1970) Design of an On-Site Evaluation System for the Office of Legal Services of the Office of Economic Opportunity. Washington, D.C.: Urban Institute.

GUILFORD, J. P. (1956) Fundamental Statistics in Psychology and Education. New York: McGraw-Hill.

——— (1954) Psychometric Methods. New York: McGraw-Hill.

Health, Education, and Welfare Department (1964) The Extension of Legal Services to the Poor. Washington, D.C.: Government Printing Office.

JARMEL, E. (1972) Legal Representation of the Poor. New York: Matthew Bender.

KEMENY, J., J. L. SNELL and G. THOMPSON (1969) Introduction to Finite Mathematics. Englewood Cliffs, N.J.: Prentice Hall.

Kettelle Corporation, John D. (1971) Evaluation of Office of Economic Opportunity Legal Services Program—Final Report. Washington, D.C.: OEO Evaluation Division.

KLAUS, W. (1972) "Legal Services Program: reply to Vice President Agnew." American Bar Association Journal 58 (November): 1178-1181.

LAIDLAW, C. (1972) Linear Programming for Urban Development Plan Evaluation. New York: Praeger.

Law in Action (1969a) 3 (January).

Law in Action (1969b) 3 (April).

LLEWELLYN, R. (1962) Linear Programming. Reading, Mass.: Addison-Wesley.

MAYO, L. and E. JONES (1964) "Legal-policy decision process: alternative thinking and the predictive function." George Washington Law Review 33 (October): 318-456.

MCKEAN, R. (1958) Efficiency in Government through Systems Analysis. New York: John Wiley.

MILLER, D. and M. STARR (1960) Executive Decisions and Operations Research. Englewood Cliffs, N.J.: Prentice Hall.

NAGEL, S. (1969) The Legal Process from a Behavioral Perspective. Homewood, Ill.: Dorsey Press.

RICHMOND, S. (1968) Operations Research for Management Decisions. New York: Ronald Press.

SAMUELSON, P. (1967) Economics: An Introductory Analysis. New York: McGraw-Hill.

SEMMEL, H. (1970) "Allocating limited resources: the case load problem" in Social Justice through Law. Mineola, N.Y.: Foundation Press.

STUMPF, H. (1973) Lawyers and the Poor. Beverly Hills, Ca.: Sage Publications.

TULLOCK, G. (1971) The Logic of the Law. New York: Basic Books.

VAJDA, S. (1961) Mathematical Programming. Reading, Mass.: Addison-Wesley.

WAGNER, H. (1969) Principles of Operations Research with Applications to Managerial Decisions. Englewood Cliffs, N.J.: Prentice Hall.

APPENDIX

This appendix deals with some matters that cut across Figures 1, 2, and 3 in the text. These points were more clearly recognized by the author after completion of the monograph.

A "point D" could be shown in Figures 2 and 3 (as it is, in fact, shown in Figure 1). This point represents the empirical position of the average agency as contrasted to optimum positions A and B (reflecting goals of minimum cost and maximum satisfaction respectively) and as contrasted to the "malimum" or worst position C (where costs are maximized and satisfaction is minimized within the feasible region). This empirical D point corresponds to a $L and $6.16 (or 9 percent of the average budget), a $C of $62.18 (or 91 percent of the average budget), a TC of $68.34, and an S of about 6.50 which is close to malimum point C.

One might ask for an explanation of the deviation between empirical point D and optimum points A and B. The answer, in general terms, is simply that the average agency budget is not being allocated efficiently between law reform and case handling in light of the relative evaluation of these two alternative activities by the OEO evaluators. More specifically, many agencies probably shy away from additional law reform work because it is more time consuming, more controversial, less frequently requested by individual clients, and more difficult to perform.

A "point E" might also be mentioned—where in Figures 1 and 2 the maximum satisfaction line and the minimum total cost line intersect, thereby maximizing benefits and minimizing costs simultaneously. At that point in Figure 1, $L = $20.41, $C = $41.09, TC = $61.50, and S = 12.00. (The values of $L and $C were found by solving for $L and $C in the pair of simultaneous equations $61.50 = $L + $C, and 12.00 − 6.29 = .34 $L − .03 $C.) In Figure 2, $L = $23.76, $C = $37.74, TC = $61.50, and S = 12.00. (These values of $L and $C were found by solving for $L and $C in the pair of simultaneous equations $61.50 = $L + $C, and $12.00/14 = \sqrt[3]{\$L} / \sqrt[3]{\$C}$.) The "super-optimum" point E, however, is to the left of the feasible region in that it allows for more than 20 percent $L and less than 80 percent $C. There is no such super-optimum intersection point in Figure 3 given the negative relation in Figure 3 between $L and $C in achieving a constant level of satisfaction.

An even greater super-optimum point F exists in Figures 1 and 2 where nothing or $.01 is spent on $C, and just enough is spent on $L to provide 12.00 (or 7.00) units of satisfaction at a cost quite substantially below $61.50. The value of $L for such a point F can be found by solving for $L in the equations 12.00 = 6.29 + (.34 · $L) + (.03 · 0), and $12.00 = 14 · \sqrt[3]{\$L} / \sqrt[3]{.01}$. The constraints, however, prevent such a solution because when the constraints are exceeded, the satisfaction equations no longer hold. To achieve 12.00 or 7.00 units while only spending .01 for $C in Figure 3 would require spending far more than the maximum $68.34 for $L given the negative and curvilinear relation in Figure 3 between $L and $C in achieving a constant level of satisfaction.

Where would the optimum points A and B be within the feasible region if the size or direction of the regression weights of $L and $C were to change in the satisfaction equation? So long as the regression weight of $L is larger than the regression weight of $C in the satisfaction equation, then the benefit maximization point will be on the minimum $C line as high as one can go without going above the maximum $L line or the maximum S line whichever comes first. Likewise the cost minimization line will also be on the minimum $C line as low as one can go without going below the minimum $L line or the minimum S line whichever comes first. On the other hand, if the regression weight of $L is smaller than the regression weight of $C, then the benefit maximization point will be on the minimum $L line as far to the right as one can go without exceeding the maximum $C line or the maximum S line whichever comes first. Likewise the cost minimization line will also be on the minimum $L line—as far to the left as one can go without exceeding the minimum $C line, or the minimum S line, whichever comes first.

Slight differences between the results shown in this paper, and the results obtainable from the quantities given herein, are due to the fact that the quantities given are generally rounded from the more precise original quantities from which the results shown are calculated.

STUART S. NAGEL *is Professor of Political Science at the University of Illinois and a member of the Illinois bar. He is the author of* The Legal Process from a Behavioral Perspective *(1969) and the forthcoming* Effects of Alternative Legal Policies, *as well as numerous journal articles and chapters in books. Dr. Nagel edited* The Rights of the Accused: in Law and Action *(Volume I, in the Sage Criminal Justice System Annuals). He has been a Yale Russell Sage Fellow in Law and Social Science and a Fellow of the Center for Advanced Study in the Behavioral Sciences. For three years he was the attorney-director of the OEO Legal Services Agency of Champaign County.*

A Better Way of Getting New Information

Research, survey and policy studies that say what needs to be said—
no more, no less.

The Sage Papers Program

Five regularly-issued original paperback series that bring, at an unusually
low cost, the timely writings and findings of the international scholarly
community. Since the material is updated on a continuing basis, each
series rapidly becomes a unique repository of vital information.

Authoritative, and frequently seminal, works that NEED to be available

- To scholars and practitioners
- In university and institutional libraries
- In departmental collections
- For classroom adoption

Sage Professional Papers

COMPARATIVE POLITICS SERIES
INTERNATIONAL STUDIES SERIES
ADMINISTRATIVE AND POLICY STUDIES SERIES
AMERICAN POLITICS SERIES

Sage Policy Papers

THE WASHINGTON PAPERS

SAGE PUBLICATIONS
The Publishers of Professional Social Science
Beverly Hills • London

Sage Professional Papers in **Comparative Politics**

Editors: Harry Eckstein, *Princeton University,* Ted Robert Gurr, *Northwestern University,* and Aristide R. Zolberg, *University of Chicago.*

VOLUME 1 (1970)

01-001 **J.Z. Namenwirth & H. D. Lasswell,** The changing language of American values: a computer study of selected party platforms $2.50/£1.05

01-002 **K. Janda,** A conceptual framework for the comparative analysis of political parties $1.90/£.80

01-003 **K. Thompson,** Cross-national voting behavior research $1.50/£.60

01-004 **W. B. Quandt,** The comparative study of political elites $2.00/£.85

01-005 **M. C. Hudson,** Conditions of political violence and instability $1.90/£.80

01-006 **E. Ozbudun,** Party cohesion in western democracies $3.00/£1.30

01-007 **J. R. Nellis,** A model of developmental ideology in Africa $1.40/£.55

01-008 **A. Kornberg,** et al., Semi-careers in political organizations $1.40/£.55

01-009 **F. I. Greenstein & S. Tarrow,** Political orientations of children $2.90/£1.25

01-010 **F. W. Riggs,** Administrative reform and political responsiveness: a theory of dynamic balance $1.50/£.60

01-011 **R. H. Donaldson & D. J. Waller,** Stasis and change in revolutionary elites: a comparative analysis of the 1956 Central Party Committees in China and the USSR $1.90/£.80

01-012 **R. A. Pride,** Origins of democracy: a cross-national study of mobilization, party systems and democratic stability $2.90/£1.25

VOLUME II (1971)

01-013 **S. Verba,** et al., The modes of democratic participation $2.80/£1.20

01-014 **W. R. Schonfeld,** Youth and authority in France $2.80/£1.20

01-015 **S. J. Bodenheimer,** The ideology of developmentalism $2.40/£1.00

01-016 **L. Sigelman,** Modernization and the political system $2.50/£1.05

01-017 **H. Eckstein,** The evaluation of political performance: problems and dimensions $2.90/£1.25

01-018 **T. Gurr & M. McLelland,** Political performance: a twelve nation study $2.90/£1.25

01-019 **R. F. Moy,** A computer simulation of democratic political development $2.70/£1.15

01-020 **T. Nardin,** Violence and the state $2.70/£1.15

01-021 **W. Ilchman,** Comparative public administration and "conventional wisdom" $2.40/£1.00

01-022 **G. Bertsch,** Nation-building in Yugoslavia $2.25/£.95

01-023 **R. J. Willey,** Democracy in West German trade unions $2.40/£1.00

01-024 **R. Rogowski & L. Wasserspring,** Does political development exist? Corporatism in old and new societies $2.40/£1.00

VOLUME III (1972)

01-025 **W. T. Daly,** The revolutionary $2.10/£.90

01-026 **C. Stone,** Stratification and political change in Trinidad and Jamaica $2.10/£.90

01-027 **Z. Y. Gitelman,** The diffusion of political innovation: from Eastern Europe to the Soviet Union $2.50/£1.05

01-028 **D. P. Conradt,** The West German party system $2.40/£1.00

01-029 **J. R. Scarritt,** Political development and culture change theory [Africa] $2.50/£1.05

01-030 **M. D. Hayes,** Policy outputs in the Brazilian states $2.25/£.95

01-031 **B. Stallings,** Economic dependency in Africa and Latin America $2.50/£1.05

01-032 **J. T. Campos & J. F. McCamant,** Cleavage shift in Colombia: analysis of the 1970 elections $2.90/£1.2

01-033 **G. Field & J. Higley,** Elites in developed societies [Norway] $2.25/£.95

01-034 **J. S. Szyliowicz,** A political analysis of student activism [Turkey] $2.80/£1.20

01-035 **E. C. Hargrove,** Professional roles in society and government [England] $2.90/£1.25

01-036 **A. J. Sofranko & R. J. Bealer,** Unbalanced modernization and domestic instability $2.90/£1.25

VOLUME IV (1973)

01-037 **W. A. Cornelius,** Political learning among the migrant poor $2.90/£1.

01-038 **J. W. White,** Political implications of cityward migration [Japan] $2.50/£1.05

01-039 **R. B. Stauffer,** Nation-building in a global economy: the role of the multi-national corporation $2.25/£.95

01-040 **A. Martin,** The politics of economic policy in the U.S. $2.50/£1.05

Forthcoming, summer/fall 1973

01-041 **M. B. Welfling,** Political Institutionalization [African party systems] $2.70*/£1.15

01-042 **B. Ames,** Rhetoric and reality in a militarized regime [Brazil] $2.40*/£1.00

01-043 **E. C. Browne,** Coalition theories $2.90*/£1.25

01-044 **M. Barrera,** Information and ideology: a study of Arturo Frondizi $2.40*/£1.00

*denotes tentative price

Papers 01-045 through 01-048 to be announ